Virgo

Also by Sally Kirkman

Aries
Taurus
Gemini
Cancer
Leo
Libra
Scorpio
Sagittarius
Capricorn
Aquarius
Pisces

SALLY KIRKMAN

Virgo

The Art of Living Well and Finding
Happiness According to Your Star Sign

HODDER

First published in Great Britain in 2018 by Hodder & Stoughton
An Hachette UK company

1

A CIP catalogue record for this title is available from the British Library

Hardback ISBN 978 1 473 67661 9

Typeset in Celeste 11.5/17 pt by Palimpsest Book Production Limited,
Falkirk, Stirlingshire

Printed in the United States of America by LSC Communications

Hodder & Stoughton policy is to use papers that are natural,
renewable and recyclable products and made from wood grown in
sustainable forests. The logging and manufacturing processes are expected
to conform to the environmental regulations of the country of origin.

Hodder & Stoughton Ltd
Carmelite House
50 Victoria Embankment
London EC4Y 0DZ

www.hodder.co.uk

Contents

• • • • •

Introduction

• • • • •

Before computers, books or a shared language, people were fascinated by the movement of the stars and planets. They created stories and myths around them. We know that the Babylonians were one of the first people to record the zodiac, a few hundred years BC.

In ancient times, people experienced a close connection to the earth and the celestial realm. The adage 'As above, so below', that the movement of the planets and stars mirrored life on earth and human affairs, made perfect sense. Essentially, we were all one, and ancient people sought symbolic meaning in everything around them.

We are living in a very different world now, in

which scientific truth is paramount; yet many people are still seeking meaning. In a world where you have an abundance of choice, dominated by the social media culture that allows complete visibility into other people's lives, it can be hard to feel you belong or find purpose or think that the choices you are making are the right ones.

It's this calling for something more, the sense that there's a more profound truth beyond the objective and scientific, that leads people to astrology and similar disciplines that embrace a universal truth, an intuitive knowingness. Today astrology has a lot in common with spirituality, meditation, the Law of Attraction, a desire to know the cosmic order of things.

Astrology means 'language of the stars' and people today are rediscovering the usefulness of ancient wisdom. The universe is always talking to you; there are signs if you listen and the more you tune in, the more you feel guided by life. This is one of astrology's significant benefits, helping you to make sense of an increasingly unpredictable world.

Used well, astrology can guide you in making the best possible decisions in your life. It's an essential skill in your personal toolbox that enables you to navigate the ups and downs of life consciously and efficiently.

About this book

Astrology is an ancient art that helps you find meaning in the world. The majority of people to this day know their star sign, and horoscopes are growing increasingly popular in the media and online.

The modern reader understands that star signs are a helpful reference point in life. They not only offer valuable self-insight and guidance, but are indispensable when it comes to understanding other people, and living and working together in harmony.

This new and innovative pocket guide updates the ancient tradition of astrology to make it relevant and topical for today. It distils the wisdom of the star signs into an up-to-date format that's easy to read and digest, and fun and informative too. Covering a broad range of topics, it offers you insight and understanding into many different areas of your life. There are some unique sections you won't find anywhere else.

The style of the guide is geared towards you being able to maximise your strengths, so you can live well and use your knowledge of your star sign to your advantage. The more in tune you are with your zodiac sign, the higher your potential to lead a happy and fulfilled life.

The guide starts with a quick introduction to your star sign, in bullet point format. This not only reveals your star sign's ancient ruling principles, but brings astrology up-to-date, with your star sign mission, an appropriate quote for your sign and how best to describe your star sign in a tweet.

The first chapter is called 'Be True To Your Sign' and is one of the most important sections in the guide. It's a comprehensive look at all aspects of your star sign, helping define what makes you special, and explaining how the rich symbolism of your zodiac sign can reveal more about your character. For example, being born at a specific time of year and in a particular season is significant in itself.

This chapter focuses in depth on the individual attributes of your star sign in a way that's positive and uplifting. It offers a holistic view of your sign and is meant to inspire you. Within this section, you find out the reasons why your star sign traits and characteristics are unique to you.

There's a separate chapter towards the end of the guide that takes this star sign information to a new level. It's called 'Your Cosmic Gifts and Talents' and tells you what's individual about you from your star sign perspective. Most importantly, it highlights your skills and strengths, offering you clear examples of how to make the most of your natural birthright.

The guide touches on another important aspect of your star sign, in the chapters entitled 'Your Shadow Side' and 'Your Star Sign Secrets'. This reveals the potential weaknesses inherent within your star sign, and the tricks and habits you can fall into if you're not aware of them. The star sign secrets might surprise you.

There's guidance here about what you can focus on to minimise the shadow side of your star sign, and this is linked in particular to your opposite sign of the zodiac. You learn how opposing forces complement each other when you hold both ends of the spectrum, enabling them to work together.

Essentially, the art of astrology is about how to find balance in your life, to gain a sense of universal or cosmic order, so you feel in flow rather than pulled in different directions.

Other chapters in the guide provide revealing information about your love life and sex life. There are cosmic tips on how to work to your star sign strengths so you can attract and keep a fulfilling relationship, and lead a joyful sex life. There's also a guide to your love compatibility with all twelve star signs.

Career, money and prosperity is another essential section in the guide. These chapters offer you vital information on your purpose in life, and how to make the most of your potential out in the world. Your star sign skills and strengths are revealed, including what sort of job or profession suits you.

There are also helpful suggestions about what to avoid and what's not a good choice for you. There's a list of traditional careers associated with your star sign, to give you ideas about where you can excel in life if you require guidance on your future direction.

Also, there are chapters in the book on practical matters, like your health and well-being, your food and diet. These recommend the right kind of exercise for you, and how you can increase your vitality and nurture your mind, body and soul, depending on your star sign. There are individual yoga poses and tarot cards that have been carefully selected for you.

Further chapters reveal unique star sign information about your image and style. This includes whether there's a particular fashion that suits you, and how you can accentuate your look and make the most of your body.

There are even chapters that can help you decide where to go on holiday and who with, and how to decorate your home. There are some fun sections, including ideal gifts for your star sign, and ideas for films, books and music specific to your star sign.

Also, the guide has a comprehensive birthday section so you can find out which famous people share your birthday. You can discover who else is born under your star sign, people who may be your role models and whose careers or gifts you can aspire to. There are celebrity examples throughout the guide too, revealing more about the unique characteristics of your star sign.

At the end of the guide, there's a Question and Answer section, which explains the astrological terms used in the guide. It also offers answers to some general questions that often arise around astrology.

This theme is continued in a useful section entitled Additional Information. This describes the symmetry of astrology and shows you how different patterns connect the twelve star signs. If you're a beginner to astrology, this is your next stage, learning about the elements, the modes and the houses.

View this book as your blueprint, your guide to you and your future destiny. Enjoy discovering astrological revelations about you, and use this pocket guide to learn how to live well and find happiness according to your star sign.

A QUICK GUIDE TO VIRGO

• • • • •

Virgo Birthdays: 23 August to 22 September

Zodiac Symbol: The Virgin

Ruling Planet: Mercury

Mode/Element: Mutable Earth

Colour: Natural earthy colours – light brown, leaf green, corn yellow

Part of the Body: Intestines, digestive and nervous system

Day of the Week: Wednesday

Top Traits: Resourceful, Attentive, Body-conscious

Your Star Sign Mission: to be a standard-bearer for excellence; to choose to sacrifice personal needs to be of service

Best At: playing a supportive role, working diligently, being efficient and effective, politeness and courtesy, daily habits, smart decisions, prioritising self-care, valuing the simple life

Weaknesses: fussy, a worrier, overly critical, self-deprecating, too literal, loses sight of the big picture

Key Phrase: I craft

Virgo Quote: 'The first thing I do in the morning is brush my teeth and sharpen my tongue.' Dorothy Parker

How to describe Virgo in a Tweet: Perfectionist with an eye for detail. Can be critical of self & others. Prim & proper on the outside; naughty & nice on the inside

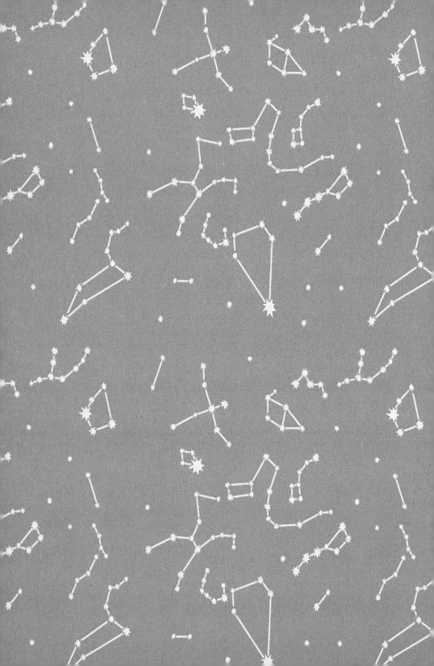

Be True To Your Sign

• • • • •

Discerning and discreet, Virgo is the perfectionist of the zodiac who favours attention to detail over the bigger picture. Your hard-work ethic reaches into all areas of your life, and you're as fastidious about your health as you are keen to educate your mind. A typical Virgo is supportive, kind, attentive and polite.

In the northern hemisphere, your birthday falls at a point in the year when the summer holidays are coming to an end and it's time to start thinking about work, and returning to a settled and routine way of life.

In Virgo season, the excesses of summer are behind you. You understand the importance of paying attention once more to your lifestyle and health, of being useful and of service and creating a framework in your life that is efficient and works well.

There's a 'back to school' vibe about your sign, which is perfect for someone who's rarely happier than when choosing stationery and pens, and positively enjoys filing and getting organised.

You like the structure of routine, and the opportunity to make lists, declutter and pin up important dates and notes. Your lively mind can focus better when you know what's happening when, and your body and thought processes function at optimum potential.

You are one of two signs of the zodiac ruled by Mercury, the planet that's associated with the mind and communication. Where you excel is the written word, which is why you are a natural list-maker, and you like to get your thoughts and ideas out of your mind and on to paper or your laptop.

If you had your whole life set out in front of you on a spreadsheet, this would be Virgo perfection, and save you a lot of worry and anxiety. You don't like to be seen as forgetful; you tend to create a busy and active lifestyle for yourself and, more often than not, you set yourself incredibly high expectations and standards. You are more critical of yourself than you are of other people.

Your need to be productive and your practical skills are linked to the fact that Virgo is one of the hands-on earth signs. Like all of these signs, you're willing to put in the work that's necessary to achieve substantial results.

Being an earth sign is helpful for someone whose ruling planet is lively Mercury because it slows you down. You take your time, you focus your mind and you are appreciative and attentive to the details of life.

You want to stop and smell the roses, rather than charge past at full tilt looking for the next experience. Being an earth sign, you are sensual and savour the richness and fullness of life.

Virgo season is synonymous with the harvest, as your birthday takes place when the full bloom of summer begins to wane and fruit and crops require picking and storing. This is the time of year to create order in the garden of life, to weed out what's useful from what's not, to get rid of the dead wood and to pack away and preserve what will come in handy at a later date.

This is where the discerning side of your nature comes into its own, and you excel at tasks where you can classify and analyse, sort and sift. You have a keen eye for assessment, for being diligent and orderly and working out how to make the best use of the resources and time available to you.

Your zodiac symbol, the Virgin, is also associated with the harvest as she is often depicted with an ear of corn in her hands. Thus, you were born to sort the wheat from the chaff.

The Virgin is the only female symbol in the zodiac and nature, in its role as 'mother earth', correlates with the feminine. Classic feminine qualities are kindness and caring, receptivity and nurturing, all traits linked to your sign.

If you are a classic Virgo, you are in tune with the laws of nature. The natural world runs to set rules and guidelines that are regular and constant. You too feel more settled and secure when your own life has a natural balance and rhythm to it.

You often feel more in flow when you wake and sleep in sync with the Sun's rise and fall. When you feel grounded, and you have regular habits in your life that support you, this refines your clarity of thought, and your sense of judgement and instinctive responses to life are spot on.

You are one of the introverted signs of the zodiac, traditionally quiet and patient, modest and unpretentious. You appreciate beauty in all its forms and, at your best, you have an innate sense of gratitude for all that life bestows upon you.

In astrology, Virgo rules the sixth house, relating to work and routine, lifestyle and health, and service to others. These are all significant areas to focus on, to perfect. When the basics are working well for you, and you are productive, healthy and useful, everything else begins to fall into place.

The sixth house is the last of the personal houses, before the turn of the astrology wheel moves out into the world. It's the halfway point round the zodiac, an ideal time to stop and assess where you've come from, where you're heading and how to be most effective and efficient moving forward.

This is another Virgo aptitude, the ability to take your time to consolidate your position, to review what you've learned, to be thorough and reflective before you continue on a chosen path.

This is necessary because you are the worker bee of the zodiac, always busy and active. In addition, you have an inbuilt skill for discrimination and assessment that means you give careful thought and attention to whatever you're involved in.

Add to this an intelligent brain and skilled hands, and you have all the tools available to you to work towards mastery in whichever craft or talent you choose to pursue. Purity, innocence and simplicity are hallmarks of the Virgo archetype, and whatever you turn your hand to or your mind towards, you will do it to the best of your ability.

Your Shadow Side

One of the archetypes of your sign of Virgo is the critic, and there are some crucial reasons why. Your attention to detail is second to none, your ability to scrutinise and analyse verges on perfection and you are naturally gifted when it comes to words, and extremely capable of expressing your thoughts eloquently.

What you do have to be careful of, however, is indulging these traits so much that you become controlling, or allow your Virgo nature to take hold to such an extent that you become a pedant.

What's worse is if you turn into a nag and your attentiveness switches to nit-picking and constant criticism. Picking up on every tiny detail is not only hard for someone else to hear but exhausting for you too. If you find you're continually complaining, moaning or getting annoyed, your shadow side has kicked in, and it's time to rein in your inner critic.

There is another possibility here too, which is when your perfectionism turns on yourself or takes over your life. As a Virgo, you tend to be self-deprecating and put yourself down whenever you don't meet your own high standards.

At its worst, this behaviour can be paralysing, because under the eye of your strict inner critic, you are never good enough, and never ready for your next move. What happens is that you start to procrastinate because, if you can't make the right decision or do something correctly, you'd rather not do it at all.

You talk the talk, in true Virgo fashion, but when it comes to walking the walk, you're immobile. If this happens, you need to loosen up and use your critical faculties to improve your life and the lives of others, rather than be a slave to your own perfectionism.

As a Virgo, you can get so caught up in the minutiae of life that you don't have any time left for fun or doing the things in life that matter and make a difference. You'll know when your shadow side kicks in if, for example, you cancel a night out because you decide it's more important to stay home and tidy your cupboards. If this happens, it's time to tell your inner critic and party pooper where to get off, politely of course.

This is where it can help to learn from your opposite sign of Pisces, as all opposite signs of the zodiac complement each other. Pisces is the boundless sign ruled by big planet Jupiter, opposite to your Mercury-motivated attention to detail. Pisces knows how to dream, how to reach for the big vision in life and access a higher purpose.

When this is in place in your life, you don't get lost in the details, and you have time and motivation to focus on what's important rather than what you perceive as urgent. When you learn from your opposite sign of Pisces, you fuss less and go with the flow of life. Sometimes, you need to stress less and chill more.

Your Star Sign Secrets

Shhh, don't tell anyone but your greatest fear is the unknown. The unknown is a vast universe, a black hole that arouses fear or trepidation, excitement or anticipation, but is anathema to your Virgo control-freak nature. Venturing forward without knowledge of the facts or a manual to guide you isn't easy for you. Plus, it arouses strong emotions within your Virgo psyche that feel uncomfortable, because you don't have the answers and you don't have everything under your control. Your dislike of the unknown is Virgo's star sign secret.

You have another secret too; that, underneath the demure and respectable exterior, there's a wild child desperately trying to get out. This Virgo character is amoral, a rule-breaker and more than ready to go screeching off the rails of life and do crazy and unimaginable stuff. You are one of the dual-natured mutable signs of the zodiac, and every now and again, prim and proper Virgo lets their inner wild child twin out for the night.

Your Love Life

Knowing about your star sign is an absolute essential when it comes to love and relationships. Once you understand what drives you, nurtures you and keeps you happy in love, then you can be true to who you are rather than try to be someone you're not.

Plus, once you recognise your weak points when it comes to relationships (and everyone has them), you can learn to moderate them and focus instead on boosting your strengths to find happiness in love.

KEY CONCEPTS: choosing the right partner, taking the sensible option, attentive and loyal, small gestures, not confusing service with love

Cosmic Tip: Old-fashioned values unlock your Virgo heart; you expect a proper courtship and hold in high esteem the tradition of asking for the hand in marriage.

Love can be a strange concept for you as a Virgo because it's not logical. Losing yourself in love, falling head-over-heels in love, meeting your dream partner: all of these possibilities can be quickly dismissed by the ever-rational Virgo mind as impossible emotional fantasies.

This can be an issue for you when it comes to love and relationships because you are often the opposite of the dashing romantic hero or heroine who will give everything up for love. Instead, you take the sensible option in life, and you need to have a good reason for entering into a relationship. Why on earth would you throw everything away on a whim?

That's sensible Virgo talking, although there is another side to your nature, which secretly wants to be whisked off your feet and loves romantic books and movies. You have a wistful character that yearns for love and romance, and to meet the perfect partner.

Where to meet someone is an interesting conundrum, because ideally you want a partner who's intelligent and bright, and who looks after themselves. Bumping into someone on a boozy night out with your mates isn't a guaranteed route to love satisfaction.

You could choose to join a club and find someone who pursues a similar interest to yourself. You might meet someone when you're in the gym, or on a yoga course, or improving yourself on a personal development workshop. The brain is a sexy organ for Virgo and, ideally, you want a partner who takes good care of their body, mind and soul.

You're not usually the type to rush into love until you find someone worth pursuing. Even then, you might turn up to a date with a long list of potential-partner criteria. Yes, it is worth holding out for someone who's going to make you happy, but approaching a date as you would a job interview can be off-putting, especially if the other person gets wind of what you're up to.

Be attentive in your search for the right relationship, but don't forget that people are rarely perfect, and all human beings come with flaws and make mistakes. If you're with a person who has decent traditional values, works hard for a living, is loyal and trustworthy and loves you for who you are, that's good enough.

If they also have poetry in their soul and can make you laugh and smile and keep you entertained, you're onto a winner. You are a sensitive soul yourself, but you rarely wear your heart on your sleeve, as you worry that emotions will blur your clear thinking.

In love, you are an attentive partner, and you usually put a lot of thought into your relationship and will work hard at making sure you get things right. Even though you're not one for grand gestures, you recognise the importance of the little things: the hugs, the 'I love you's', the thoughtful gifts.

You do have certain standards that can't be broken. For example, it can be hard for you living with someone who's chaotic or slobbish all the time, and vulgarity and rudeness are definite turn-offs.

This is when you need to watch your critical tongue. It's easy for you to pick up on the smallest of details, which can then quickly escalate and send love askew. Be accommodating in love, and learn to recognise when to go with the flow and when to pull someone up for their behaviour.

Also, take care that you don't put your partner's needs entirely before your own. If you start to feel unappreciated in a relationship, you wilt like a flower and, once you begin to feel unloved, you grow quiet and shut down. Be careful that you don't blame yourself entirely for a relationship breakdown, and don't allow your self-deprecating Virgo voice to take hold.

In this situation, what's needed is to get back in touch with your passion. Get angry if necessary, rather than allow yourself to be a doormat. Have people in your life who remind you of your strengths, and refuse to put up with a relationship that makes you feel weak.

There is a side to your Virgo nature that would put up with an affair. As long as it works for you, and the affair gives you what you need, do whatever makes you happy. The same goes if you choose not to be in a relationship, which, at specific times in your life, is an option for your sign.

You are one of life's givers, and the iconic role of the Japanese geisha fits the Virgo symbolism. The traditional definition of the geisha is a female entertainer who is skilled in various performing arts, such as dance, classical music and conversation. Their role is to be attentive and care for their client's every need. The geisha is not submissive or subservient, however, but is honoured and revered for her skill and strength.

As a Virgo, you can perhaps learn something from this analogy. Take your particular strengths and gifts into a loving relationship, be attentive and skilled and ensure that in return, you're honoured and revered entirely, by a partner who worships the ground you walk on.

Your Love Matches

Some star signs are a better love match for you than others. The classic combinations are the other two star signs from the same element as your sign, earth; in Virgo's case, Taurus and Capricorn.

These are the sensible options, and excellent for a sensual and serious long-term relationship. If, however, you want a relationship to bring out your wild child, look for someone who's spontaneous, confident and full of life.

It's also important to recognise that any star sign match can be a good match if you're willing to learn from each other and use astrological insight to understand more about what makes the other person tick. Here's a quick guide to your love matches with all twelve star signs:

Virgo–Aries: Soulmates

Virgo and Aries, the Virgin meets the Ram. You are inherently different in personality; your sign loves order while Aries is wild. This combination can unleash hidden depths and passion. A lasting relationship, however, requires patience and less criticism from both sides.

Virgo–Taurus: In Your Element

Routine and security are essential for both of you, and there's a mutual appreciation of what money can buy. You share a love of good food. A sensual match, you are both body-oriented, and affection and hands-on touching create a pleasurable and happy relationship.

Virgo–Gemini: Squaring Up To Each Other

You two share the same ruling planet, Mercury, lover of all things chatty, intelligent and versatile. Together you are fun, witty and slightly eccentric. If it feels like you're best mates rather than lovers, turn to a self-help manual and spice up your sex life to keep the romance alive.

Virgo–Cancer: Sexy Sextiles

You two are not only super-caring but fundamentally happy to lead a routine lifestyle. You enjoy taking care of each other – but do avoid moaning. The little things in life make the most significant difference, and there's no shortage of cuddle sessions in this comfy combination.

Virgo–Leo: Next-Door Neighbours

This love match is all about looking and feeling good. Your sign of Virgo enjoys living life to the full with fun-loving Leo, and Leo adores the attention that you can offer them. If you can balance work and play and keep the spark of love alive, you two can make a winning team.

Virgo–Virgo: Two Peas In A Pod

This is a prim and proper pairing as you are sticklers for etiquette and doing things right. Even falling in love needs to be approached correctly, with due thought and attention. Criticism could be your undoing, but learning to accept each other for who you are is the key to lasting love.

Virgo–Libra: Next-Door Neighbours

A refined and cultured match, this is a romantic pairing. Both you and Libra appreciate beauty and order and enjoy sampling the more elegant things in life. A meeting of minds and a healthy work/life balance is on the cards when you learn to appreciate each other fully.

Virgo–Scorpio: Sexy Sextiles

You two pay attention to the details, but you share OCD tendencies. Your high standards meet Scorpio's laser focus, and you can get lost in detail rather than focusing on the bigger picture. You both have hidden depths. Once unleashed this can be a hotbed of pulsating passion.

Virgo–Sagittarius: Squaring Up To Each Other

Virgo is the god of small things, whereas Sagittarius rules everything big and expansive. You must allow Sagittarius full rein to roam free, and Sagittarius must pay attention to your everyday wants and needs. Get the balance right, and you two can be bigger and better together.

Virgo–Capricorn: In Your Element

You share a hard-work ethic, and this partnership can be as successful in business as in love. A sense of ambition and working towards common goals helps create a close bond between you. Work together in harmony and focus on a shared awareness of the mind–body–spirit connection.

Virgo–Aquarius: Soulmates

Virgo and Aquarius meet on an intellectual plane. Two of the most intelligent and studious signs of the zodiac, you two can be best friends as well as lovers. Sharing an interest in social and environmental concerns helps keep the spark of love alive.

Virgo–Pisces: Opposites Attract

You are the list-maker, the perfectionist who thrives on routine and order. Pisces is the poet, the mystic, a soft touch. Together you can teach one another about compassion and serve humanity. Finding a shared romantic muse becomes your inspiration for creativity and magic.

Your Sex Life

• • • • •

Your zodiac symbol is the Virgin, and even your zodiac glyph, the character that represents your sign, looks like you have your legs crossed. Add to this the fact that you have a reputation for being prim and proper, and it's no wonder that other people don't expect you to be overly interested in sex.

This is not necessarily the truth, although there is a side of your Virgo nature that's willing to sacrifice yourself for a higher purpose. Take Queen Elizabeth I (7 September), for example, who reigned in the sixteenth century. A Sun Virgo, she earned the title 'The Virgin Queen'.

One of the more positive definitions of the word 'virgin' has nothing to do with chastity, but rather describes a woman who does not need a man because she is entirely self-sufficient and self-contained. This can apply to both sexes and, as a Sun Virgo, you may at certain times in your life choose to pursue other activities unrelated to physical pleasures.

There is, however, a duality to your Virgo nature, and the ancient Roman goddess Vesta, while attended by virgins, was also a goddess of fertility and growth. So while there's a side to the Virgo character that comes across as strait-laced and untouchable, this has a lot to do with your love of dignity and decorum, rather than being prudish. You are discriminating when it comes to sex, and you pick and choose your lovers accordingly. You are fussy about who you go to bed with, and rightly so.

Cleanliness is of vital importance if you're to have good sex, and you might choose to perform a ritual of bathing or showering before you and your lover get it together. It's a similar story when it comes to the bedroom, as pristine, crisp cotton white sheets are more of a turn-on than scruffy bedding, a Virgo nightmare.

The image of the Virgo lover as cool on the outside and red-hot on the inside is reasonably accurate. You might look as if you wouldn't know your way around the bedroom, but you have a real depth of passion once it's unleashed. Earth signs like yours are sensual and thrive on affection and touching.

Plus, you want to become an expert in whatever you turn your hand to. A typical Virgo will enjoy studying the *Kama Sutra* from cover to cover and learning more than a few sexual positions. If a job's worth doing, it's worth doing well as far as you're concerned, and you'll happily study sex manuals if it's going to improve your performance and your lover's.

You're such a perfectionist that you could try a complicated sex manoeuvre again and again until you get it exactly right. Let's hope, however, that your lover is a quick learner too, as the last thing they want to hear is that they're not doing it right. Instead, take control of the situation, and use your hands and expertise to ensure there's pleasure on both sides.

VIRGO ON A FIRST DATE

- you check arrangements numerous times

- you are immaculately groomed and subtly sexy

- you expect good manners from your date

- you show off your intelligence and wit

- you are particular about how they smell and the way they eat

Your Friends and Family

Strong friendships last for ever when you're a Virgo, and you're a reliable, loyal and caring friend. Many of you share a close connection with a sibling, and once you have a strong bond or tie with someone special in your life, you will move heaven and earth to ensure that bond is never broken.

You make new friends easily too, especially if you move in circles where you meet people who are as bright and talented as yourself. When you have an active social life, and you are proactive in pursuing activities that interest you, you have lots to talk about, and you're a smart and witty conversationalist.

You are a creature of comfort, however, and a lover of routine, and it is easy for you to slip into a rut. If you get stuck in your comfort zone, some friends might leave you behind and accuse you of being boring.

It can be a similar scenario if you go through a stage in life where you can't be bothered to make an effort, and you feel fed up more often than you're happy. Some friends will be there for you if you moan and groan, but friendship, like all areas of life, is best when you bring a spark to it.

It's a good idea for you to be around people who enliven you with their spontaneity and motivation. In fact, every Virgo should have at least one wild friend in their life who knows how to awaken your inner rebel.

It's important too that you know your personality, and what you have to offer as a friend. If you're unsure of who you are, you sometimes try to model yourself on a friend. This can be flattering up to a point, as long as you don't become a total copycat or turn into a clone.

Where you excel in friendship is in your ability to solve problems and listen well. You will go out of your way to help the ones you love, and no task is too big or small for your vast well of Virgo caring and kindness.

When it comes to friendship, you might choose to steer clear of people who bring drama and chaos into your life. You don't like excessive behaviour either, but prefer to be around people who enable you to feel balanced and harmonious.

You come across as cool, and you're not usually one for emotional outbursts. Other people might think you don't care, but this isn't true. Instead, you prefer to take a step back and analyse any tricky friendship situation rationally.

One of your less attractive qualities as a friend is when you come across as a know-it-all. In fact, one of your most frequently used phrases is 'I know', because you don't like to be wrong or make a mistake. The irony is that your friends think of you as smart and know that your quick and receptive mind holds a lot of valuable knowledge and information. This is why other people often turn to you for a reality check or good advice.

When it comes to family connections, they often remain strong throughout your lifetime. Some Virgo individuals live close to home in adulthood, as routine and security are essential components of the Virgo guide to well-being and happiness. You like cosy domesticity, and you will happily stick with what you know.

There is a dutiful side to your character and, if any child is going to look after their ailing parents, it will be a Virgo. You were born to serve, but ensure that you choose to be there for the ones you love, rather than do so out of a sense of obligation, which can quickly turn into resentment.

As a Virgo, you have clear rules and guidelines by which to live, and if someone close to you doesn't agree, this can be where close relationships break down. You have your own moral code, and find it hard to come to terms with family or friends who continually break the rules.

When it comes to parenting, you understand the need for structure and routine in a child's life, and you're well-informed about every detail of the parenting process. At some point, however, you have to recognise that living by rules twenty-four seven can not only knock the fun out of life but be impossible too. If anything, having a child is an excellent lesson in learning to let go, be spontaneous and enjoy fun and laughter.

Parenting is something you often consider long and hard before you commit to it. You want to make the right decision, whether that means choosing not to have children, being a single parent or deciding on the exact number of children or adopted children for your family.

Your Health and Well-Being

> **KEY CONCEPTS:** health and diet expert, leading a stress-free lifestyle, sensitive gut, locally sourced food, being more Zen

If there's one sign of the zodiac that can be termed health-conscious, it's Virgo. This isn't surprising because Virgo rules the sixth house in astrology, linked to health and lifestyle. If you're a typical Virgo, you enjoy routine, and this includes regular exercise as well as rituals that take care of your body.

Daily habits are an integral part of Virgo's structure, and you care significantly about hygiene and body maintenance. In fact, you are often more scrupulous about your health and well-being than about any other area of your life.

Add to this your compulsive nature, and you can turn into a fitness fanatic. Whether your drug is the gym, yoga or daily walks, once you have a regular regime and it makes you feel good, you're likely to stick to it.

There is another reason, however, why you often make regular exercise part of your routine. This is because you are one of the zodiac's worriers, if not the biggest worrier. Your ruling planet is Mercury, connected to the mind; and, in the body, Virgo rules the nervous system.

Put the two together, and you have to be careful that you don't take on too much or become such a perfectionist in your endeavours that you create a lot of stress in your life. Stress is Virgo's demon, another reason why it's imperative for you to look after yourself. If you're a typical Virgo, you'll be acutely aware of the mind–body–spirit connection.

It is beneficial for you to factor relaxation and quiet times into your routine. Be more Zen and head to the hills for a walk in nature. You're one of the earth signs, so being in the countryside and breathing in the fresh air does wonders for you.

Also, your sign rules the intestines and the digestive system, and the state of your mind affects your digestion. You might have a sensitive gut and, as a Virgo, it's important for you to trust your 'gut' instincts, and listen to your body and inner knowing for clues to your health and well-being.

Many Virgo individuals become interested in complementary medicine and alternative remedies at some point in their lifetime. This can be triggered by a health crisis, or sometimes it's just your earth sign nature that draws you back to the earth for wisdom. Herbs and plants help to heal and soothe a stressed-out Virgo system.

Herbal teas and drinks are good for you, especially those that are calming and balancing, such as chamomile and valerian. Your mind sometimes races, and at its most extreme this can flip into neurosis or a hyperactive state.

Essential oils will help to calm and soothe any tension, and you tend to respond well to aroma-therapy. Lavender is your signature oil, as it can help rebalance your nervous system.

You do have something of a reputation for being a hypochondriac, but the truth is that you are sensitive to your body and pick up on anything that's out of alignment. The trick is to learn what your body, mind and soul need without letting worry take hold.

Create rituals in your life that leave you feeling rejuvenated, take up a precision sport, such as fencing, and learn to love your body without being overly fastidious. When it comes to your health and well-being, learning to trust and go with the flow benefits you immensely.

Virgo and Food

As a Virgo, you are often one of the zodiac's pickiest eaters. If you have problems with your digestion, then you will want to find out which foods work for you and which don't. Food elimination can be time-consuming, but if anyone's going to have the patience and meticulous attention to detail to make it work, it's Virgo.

Even if you are a healthy eater, you tend to experiment with different diets, as you care about the food you eat and you want to stay in good shape. You might lean towards macrobiotic food, enjoy the numbers-counting game of calories or prefer the holistic approach of an Ayurvedic diet; whatever works for you.

Many Virgo individuals follow a vegetarian or vegan diet, or perhaps you choose to fast or detox to clean out your system. Your knowledge of food and nutrition is often extensive, and you might have your own nutritionist or diet expert who gives you invaluable advice.

Virgo season coincides with the harvest, and vegetables that grow beneath the earth, such as potatoes, carrots, celeriac and fennel, are ruled by your sign. You tend to prefer natural, organic food, whether you grow your own vegetables or herbs or shop at your local farmers' market.

If you're a typical Virgo, you care about the environment and favour sustainable produce. Virgo rules grains, pulses and nuts and, as your birthday season is the precursor to autumn, wholesome soups and stews are ideal for your metabolism. If you're a meat eater, you often enjoy eating game, also ruled by Virgo and synonymous with the onset of autumn.

You usually like to cook, but the classic Virgo approach is to follow a recipe rather than make it up as you go along. You enjoy bringing people together to share food, and any form of catering always involves a lengthy and meticulously written shopping list, plus an extensive menu of small plates of food.

Excess doesn't suit your Virgo lifestyle, whether that's drinking too much alcohol or binge-eating junk food. Instead, you fare best with a moderate and healthy diet.

Do You Look Like A Virgo?

The classic Virgo comes in a perfectly formed, compact package. Your quick metabolism means you burn up energy, and you are usually of average height, rather than overly tall or short. You have a sprightly nature and a short step, and your movements are measured and precise.

You can be quite shy or reserved, so you rarely bound into a room. Instead, your natural demeanour is quiet and introverted, and you would rather wait for another person to make eye contact or speak first.

There's a classic sensuality about the Virgo look and an enigmatic quality to your facial expression. You don't give a lot away on first appearance, although your eyes are often sparkly and expressive and take everything in.

The typical Virgo face is perfectly symmetrical, and traditionally you have a high forehead, a widow's peak and delicate, thin lips. Impeccably styled hair completes a look that's elegant and neat.

Your Style and Image

The archetypal look for a Virgo woman is the prim and proper librarian, complete with twinset, tweed skirt and pearls. Admittedly you are not someone who dresses inappropriately, but there are certain myths about your sign that are untrue.

For starters, you are an earth sign, and earth is the most sensual of all the elements. Think of some classic beauties, e.g. Sophia Loren (20 September) or Raquel Welch (5 September). Both Virgo women, they are sultry and voluptuous, as is a more contemporary example, Beyoncé (4 September).

There's often a purity and wholesomeness to the Virgo look, and you like to dress impeccably, in keeping with your perfectionist streak. You are usually well groomed and coordinate your outfits, loving attention to detail and quality tailored clothes. Shoes must be shiny and make-up correct, and you add subtle accessories that complete the tasteful yet understated look. Virgo women like to wear matching sets of lingerie.

Virgo colours are muted and natural, like olive green, beige, caramel and burnt sienna. You rarely go for loud or overly bright designs, but instead favour checks and stripes, classic prints and small, repeat patterns. An excellent example of Virgo style is the fashion label Burberry, founded by a Virgo, Thomas Burberry (27 August).

Virgo men look cool and sophisticated, and there's an old-school charm to their look. They scrub up well and ooze natural style. Think of Sean Connery (25 August) in his role as James Bond, or the dashing actor Idris Elba (6 September).

Once you've found a style that suits you, it becomes something of a uniform. You're not interested in keeping up to date with fashion trends; instead, you dress correctly for every occasion. Clothes must always be clean and undamaged, although you can be happy slobbing around at home.

The archetype of the Virgo individual who wears vegan shoes, smock tops and harem pants and has excessive body hair is mostly another myth. You do, however, rock the hipster look, complete with smart vintage clothes, goatee beards and edgy hairstyles. Virgo women look good in plaits and braids too.

What typifies your Virgo style is a look that rejects extreme definitions of masculinity or femininity. You're not interested in flaunting your sex, but favour a conservative style that allows your intellect and personality to shine above your gender.

Your Home

Your Ideal Virgo Home:

An Arts and Crafts home designed from natural materials, simple and functional, with a nod to fine craftsmanship. Open-plan with wooden floors, the overall style is light and spacious, bringing the beauty and harmony of nature indoors.

You have a reputation for being obsessively tidy, but that's not true for everyone born under your sign. You do, however, usually fall into one of two categories. Either your home is a shrine to order and organisation, spotlessly clean with everything in its right place, or you go the other way and are quite happy to live in a muddle and a mess.

You prefer smaller items of furniture to anything big and bulky. You like to have objects around you that are pleasing to the eye, but mainly the Virgo style is simple and functional.

If you're a typical Virgo, you have an eye for detail, and you enjoy any object that's been beautifully constructed. It's the small, delicate touches and tasteful, refined decoration that you pick up on.

Natural materials take pride of place in the Virgo home, e.g. wood, leather and rustic materials. Virgo is an earth sign, associated with the colours of nature, such as leaf green, earth brown and corn yellow. Neutral tones are easier on the Virgo eye than anything too glaring. You like subtlety in your choice of colour.

In your home, you usually opt for a conservative yet modern style, nothing too fancy but nothing too plain either. You like decoration, and you veer towards small prints and narrow stripes in the fabrics you choose. Everything needs to be matching and coordinated, from the choice of curtains to cushion covers and even the lampshades.

You prefer a home that's easy to keep clean and lets in lots of natural light. You are very observant, however, and always notice if windows aren't pristine or where dust gathers.

If you can have herbs growing on the windowsill or indoor plants, even a conservatory, this suits your earth sign nature. You like your home to smell good, and you appreciate home fragrances or scented candles. Nature is your domain, and you are often happier in the middle of the countryside or a quiet village than a bustling town or city.

If you're a typical Virgo, you're a doer and like to keep busy. Therefore, functionality is a top concept for your living arrangements. You want storage that's practical, and you're a sucker for any invention or gadget that cuts down on clutter.

If you're the type of Virgo who enjoys growing fruit and vegetables, a pantry or larder is ideal to store your home-made jams or elderflower wine. Create a study or quiet area too, somewhere you can read and relax, and wind down. If you're the type of Virgo who views tidying as an art form, you might even colour-coordinate your books, arrange CDs or DVDs alphabetically or uniformly fold up all your socks.

Essentially, you want a home where you can shake off any stress from your day. When you look around, a sense of order and calm helps you to feel collected and composed in response.

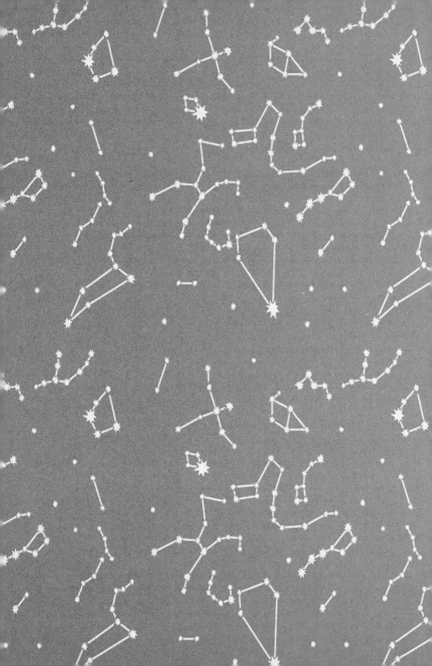

Your Star Sign Destinations

IDEAS FOR VIRGO:

• *a back-to-nature camping trip*

• *detox at a spa resort in the Alps*

• *an organised tour of classical Greece*

Did you know that many cities and countries are ruled by a particular star sign? This is based on when a country was founded, although, depending on their history, sometimes places have more than one star sign attributed to them.

This can help you decide where to go on holiday and it can also be why there are certain places where you feel at home straight away.

Virgo is the organiser of the zodiac, and wherever you head to your trip must be meticulously planned. You could happily spend hours looking at timetables and checking out hotels and sightseeing spots online. You rarely like to waste time and prefer to have every minute of the day accounted for. Holiday spreadsheet? It's a strong possibility.

For a stress-free alternative, however, why not book yourself onto an organised tour, and then you don't have to think about anything. You do, though, like to feed your mind while on holiday and learn more about the history or culture of the place you're visiting.

Usually, you prefer to go on holiday with friends or family who you get on with, and who are a good match with regard to your intellect and interests. You can let your hair down on an 18–30 style holiday once in a while, but the novelty of a holiday targeted towards booze and sex tends to wear off quickly.

Instead, you might choose a healthy holiday option or a chance for self-improvement. You like to look after yourself mind, body and soul, and simplicity and purity appeal. Holiday food also needs to be taken into account, as you like to eat well when you're away, rather than mess up your diet with chips and fried food.

A return to nature and a chance to relax, replenish and rejuvenate is always a favourite Virgo getaway. This is particularly important if you live and work in a busy city. Head for the great outdoors and breathe in the fresh air. Alternatively, a romantic weekend in Paris, one of the cities ruled by Virgo, and the city of love to boot, would come a close second.

Countries ruled by Virgo include Greece, Turkey, Iraq, Croatia

Cities ruled by Virgo include Paris, Toulouse and Lyons in France; Athens and Rhodes in Greece; Boston in the USA; Heidelberg in Germany

Your Career and Vocation

> KEY CONCEPTS: supporting role, the analyst, clear understanding, a good head for business, quiet and privacy, mastery of a craft

You are a conscientious worker and, if you're a classic Virgo, you make an excellent employee. You are one of the most reliable of people, and your quick mind combined with a clear sense of obligation and duty means you not only want to do your best but you're capable too.

Virgo isn't traditionally one of the leaders of the zodiac but, instead, you excel at playing a supporting role. You make an excellent follower because you listen attentively, you come up with intelligent solutions and you read situations well. Also, you prefer to shun the limelight rather than take centre stage.

That's not to say, however, that you can't step into a position of leadership, and you are exceptionally well suited to being a vice president or COO. Take Sheryl Sandberg (28 August), for example, Chief Operations Officer at Facebook, who's acknowledged as being a brilliant partner to CEO Mark Zuckerberg. Zuckerberg's sign of Taurus complements Sandberg's sign of Virgo, as they are both earth signs.

All earth signs excel in business. The corporate world is your domain, especially if you're in a career or profession that adheres to strict rules and guidelines. You work well in a stable structure or established company, as you like to have a safe base and stability in your working life.

You are a statistician and analyst, and you're extraordinarily capable when it comes to creating systems, dealing with large amounts of data and balancing the books. You have an excellent eye for detail, you're good with figures and you can cut through complicated processes to pick out what's most relevant or valuable. This is where your perfectionist skills come into their own, and you're often someone who's willing to stay late or put in the extra hours to ensure a job is done well.

Whatever your chosen profession, if you're able to create order from a sense of chaos you're in your element. You can tidy up after other people too, and because of your ability for discernment and discrimination, you are a complementary member of any team.

You do have to monitor your critical nature, however, and learn that the best way to give feedback is to start with something positive before you move on to anything negative. You're rarely comfortable in the company of prima donnas, particularly if they're loud and enthusiastic but don't know how to get things done.

In some respects, you are the Boy Scout of the zodiac, because you're invariably well prepared, you're practical and you are excellent at inspection and checking that things work. This is where your critical nature lends itself well. Alex Polizzi (28 August) is in the ideal profession in her role as the 'Hotel Inspector' on UK TV.

Feeling useful and being of service are both attributes that provide great fulfilment for your Virgo character. A career where you can help other people or make a difference is not only worthwhile but satisfying. You have a kind and gentle nature, whether you're nursing or caring for other people or looking after pets. Your patience and attentiveness help here too.

It is imperative, however, that you have an outlet for your lively and intelligent mind. Mercury, your ruling planet, is linked to thought processes and communication. If you're a typical Virgo, you love to study and learn and educate your mind. You pick things up quickly, and your systematic brain can help you find the insight and understanding within a whole heap of information. For this reason, you make an excellent editor or copywriter.

These skills are helpful too when it comes to coaching or teaching. You are often a wealth of useful advice and imparting what you know in easy-to-understand language can be a boon for others, and open doors in your career or vocation.

Think about hiring a coach or mentor yourself during your career, as this can boost your self-confidence. If you recognise that you thrive on encouragement, or you need someone in your life to remind you of your strengths and teach you how to show off your gifts or talents, this can be invaluable.

You know how to master a craft, and you're very willing to put in the time and hours necessary to achieve a personal goal. In fact, you often shine in a profession that benefits your introverted nature. You're not a natural people person, even though you have the gift of the gab. You often prefer a certain amount of quiet and privacy in your life, so consider these needs too when choosing a career.

Also, many Virgo individuals work in the areas of diet and health. This can be a particular focus for you in your personal life, and it's often a natural progression to pass on what you've learned about your health and well-being over the years.

If you're seeking inspiration for a new job, take a look at the following list, which reveals the traditional careers that come under the Virgo archetype:

TRADITIONAL VIRGO CAREERS

novelist

professional organiser

systems analyst

COO

auditor

PA/VA

office worker

librarian

professional cleaner

aromatherapist

herbalist

dietician

vet

ecologist

agriculturist

tailor

craftsperson

voice actor

scriptwriter

technician

Your Money and Prosperity

KEY CONCEPTS: spreadsheets and money apps, frugal nature, saving and planning for the future, crafty ways of making money

All the earth signs, Virgo included, are interested in and good at dealing with money. This is because money represents security to you. If you're a typical Virgo, you like to know where the next pay cheque is coming from, and that you have a safe base in life. If you're solvent and financially secure, it's one thing less for you to worry about.

Being a Virgo, you often take this to the next stage, because you're a natural with figures. You might draw up the most detailed budget, including a written spreadsheet or app where you monitor all your spending and expenses. You can be finicky about money matters, and you like to know exactly how much is coming in and going out, on a daily basis.

When it comes to earning money, your hard-work ethic kicks in, and you understand that being diligent and persistent creates results. Like all the earth signs, you think about the future. Your practical nature means you'll draw up long-term goals or saving schemes to finance an expensive purchase or plan for retirement.

Also, as a Virgo, you are one of the most frugal signs of the zodiac, and you can be strict with yourself and people close to you when necessary.

You are less likely to put money on credit but instead will work out ways and schemes in which to manage your finances well.

This is a sensible approach to money management, but you do need to be careful that you don't knock the fun out of life altogether. You're rarely an impulse buyer, and sometimes it takes a lot for you to be willing to spend money on entertainment, holidays or having a good time. If you deem any activity frivolous, your frugal sign means you will give yourself a good talking-to instead of allowing yourself to join in.

This is where it's worthwhile for you to learn more about your money mindset, especially the lessons you received growing up. Sometimes as a Virgo you have to learn to embrace abundance and to trust in life, that the universe will provide for you. This rarely comes naturally to you, but it can be a boon in helping you attract money and live plentifully.

You are often savvy at coming up with good ways to earn more money when needed. This is where the craft-oriented side of your nature can come into its own. You're good with your hands, whether your particular skill is writing poems, making jams and pickles, drying herbs, crocheting or knitting. Once you learn how to sell your home-made creations, perhaps in a WI-style stall at a market, this can be a tidy Virgo money-earner.

You might even take it one step further and become a successful artist like Virgo Grandma Moses (7 September), who only took up painting in earnest at the age of seventy-eight. She started selling her work cheaply but quickly began to command substantial sums of money for her art.

Grandma Moses proves it's never too late to find success and prosperity in life. A typical Virgo realist, she declared 'Life is what we make it, always has been, always will'. Sound words of advice for a Virgo.

Your Cosmic Gifts and Talents

Writing Class

You are often top of the class when it comes to writing. It's the perfect profession for a Virgo: you are a first-rate wordsmith, you enjoy time to yourself and you have excellent self-discipline.

Therefore, it's no surprise that Virgo is renowned as the author of the zodiac, and many Virgo authors are prolific writers. Here are some of the most famous: Stephen King (21 September), Roald Dahl (13 September), Agatha Christie (15 September), Paulo Coelho (24 August), Leo Tolstoy (9 September).

Supporting Role

You have the credentials to work hard at life, because you're diligent and talented, patient and persistent as you make your way to the top. You don't always have the confidence or ambition to take on a top role, and you rarely want to be in the limelight. Where you do excel, however, is using your intelligence and analytical skills in a supporting role.

This might be not in business, but elsewhere in your life. Take Pippa Middleton (6 September), for example, who swiftly became one of the world's most famous bridesmaids in her role as maid of honour at the Royal Wedding of her sister, Catherine, and Prince William in 2011.

Create Your Masterpiece

It has been estimated that it takes 10,000 hours to master a skill or talent. This requires incredible self-control and purposefulness, and you need to be adept at completing long-term goals. These are all top traits of your sign of Virgo, and when you find your passion in life, you can happily spend hours (and hours) entirely focused on learning. You might be a skilled dressmaker, a first-class interior designer, a talented pianist, a multi-linguist, a top member of Mensa; whatever your thing, be committed and create your masterpiece.

Natural Remedies

As a Virgo, you have an affinity with nature, and you like to either grow your own food, go green or go organic. Also, you often have an innate understanding of the medicinal and dietary bene-fits of herbs and plants. If you're a typical Virgo, you trust in natural remedies, and many Virgo individuals are skilled nutritionists, naturopaths or dieticians. Return to the traditional ways of nature to improve your health and the health of others, and promote healing.

Finishing School

If you're a typical Virgo, you were born with good manners, and politeness and social etiquette come naturally to you. You often have great deportment, especially when you look after your body, and you are always conscious of your demeanour and other people's behaviour in public. In fact, you can teach the rest of the zodiac a thing or two about how to behave well.

Elegance, exclusivity and charm were handed out to most Virgo individuals at birth, and you have the perfect credentials to be exacting, courteous and respectful. Some people might call you old-fashioned, but you're an excellent role model for traditional values.

Be Of Service

Your ability to help others is beyond compare, and you are often willing to be of service. In fact, you come into your own when you're useful in life and can express your kind and caring nature. An archetypal example is Mother Teresa (26 August), who was admired for her charitable work.

The sisters who joined her religious congregation took vows of chastity, poverty and obedience; all of which are Virgo traits, admittedly extreme ones. Be of service in a way that works for you personally, e.g. help out at a charity, sign up to be a volunteer, help people, care for pets or devote yourself to a religious ideal.

Eternal Youth

Your ruling planet Mercury is linked to youth and, as a Virgo, you age exceptionally well, especially when you stay active and curious about life.

Think of the classic beauties mentioned in the Style section: Sophia Loren (20 September) and Raquel Welch (5 September) continue to look stunning in their later years. Iris Apfel (29 August) is a fashion icon in her nineties who looks ridiculously young and has been called the Goddess of Style.

Virgo men too often keep their youthful looks, and good examples are Richard Gere (31 August) and Hugh Grant (9 September). Keep your mind lively and your spirit young, and take advantage of Virgo's leaning towards eternal youth.

Films, Books, Music

• • • • •

Films: The Matrix series starring Keanu Reeves (2 September) or *The Hobbit* – Bilbo Baggins (22 September) is a Virgo, as are the two actors who portrayed him, Ian Holm (12 September) and Martin Freeman (8 September)

Books: *The Fault In Our Stars* by John Green (24 August) or *Wild* by Cheryl Strayed (17 September)

Music: Cool pop stars: 'King of Pop' Michael Jackson (29 August), Freddie Mercury (5 September), Nick Cave (22 September) or Florence Welch (28 August)

YOGA POSE:

Reclining Twist: massages the abdominal
organs and aids digestion

TAROT CARD:

Temperance

GIFTS TO BUY A VIRGO:

desk lamp
personalised stationery
aromatherapy oils
indoor plants
toolkit
Egyptian cotton white bedsheets
a creative writing course
clothes for your pet
Star Gift – home gym

Virgo Celebrities Born On Your Birthday

AUGUST

22 (Dorothy Parker – born on the cusp, see Q&A)

23 River Phoenix

24 Paulo Coelho, Dave Chappelle, Jean-Michel Jarre, Stephen Fry, John Green, Rupert Grint

25 Sean Connery, Regis Philbin, Gene Simmons, Elvis Costello, Tim Burton, Billy Ray Cyrus, Claudia Schiffer, Rachel Bilson, Blake Lively, Alexandra Burke, Alexander Skarsgård, Rachael Ray, China Anne McClain

 26 Christopher Isherwood, Alison Steadman, Macaulay Culkin, Chris Pine, Melissa McCarthy, Thalia, Dylan O'Brien, Shirley Manson

 27 Mother Teresa, Chandra Wilson, Sarah Chalke, Suranne Jones, Tom Ford, Thomas Burberry, Aaron Paul, Jeanette Winterson

 28 Shania Twain, Jack Black, Jason Priestley, Jennifer Coolidge, LeAnn Rimes, Armie Hammer, Sheryl Sandberg, Ai Weiwei, Florence Welch, Alex Polizzi

 29 Ingrid Bergman, Charlie Parker, Richard Attenborough, Michael Jackson, Lenny

Henry, Liam Payne, Lea Michele, Iris
Apfel

30 Mary Shelley, Kitty Wells, Warren
Buffett, Cameron Diaz, Bebe Rexha, John
Peel

31 Queen Rania of Jordan, Maria Montessori,
James Coburn, Van Morrison, Richard
Gere, Debbie Gibson, Chris Tucker, Kirstie
Allsopp

SEPTEMBER

1 Barry Gibb, Lily Tomlin, Dr Phil McGraw,
Gloria Estefan, Jhonen Vasquez, Zendaya,
Rachel Zoe, Padma Lakshmi

2 Keanu Reeves, Lennox Lewis, Salma
Hayek

3 Alan Ladd, Pauline Collins, Charlie Sheen,
Fearne Cotton

4 Mark Ronson, Beyoncé

5 Bob Newhart, Raquel Welch, John Cage, Werner Herzog, George Lazenby, Freddie Mercury, Michael Keaton, Rose McGowan

6 Dolores O'Riordan, Tim Henman, Naomie Harris, Kerry Katona, Pippa Middleton, Idris Elba, Foxy Brown, Rosie Perez

7 Grandma Moses, Buddy Holly, Chrissie Hynde, Evan Rachel Wood, Gloria Gaynor

8 Peter Sellers, Patsy Cline, Pink, Joe Sugg, Martin Freeman, Wiz Khalifa

9 Colonel Sanders, Leo Tolstoy, Otis Redding, Hugh Grant, Adam Sandler, Julia Sawalha, Rachel Hunter, Macy Gray, Natasha Kaplinsky, Michelle Williams, Michael Bublé

10 Arnold Palmer, Karl Lagerfeld, Colin Firth, Guy Ritchie, Ryan Phillippe, Coco Rocha

11 Virginia Madsen, D.H. Lawrence, Barry Sheene, Moby, Harry Connick Jr, Ludacris, Taraji P. Henson

12 Jesse Owens, Desmond Llewelyn, Ian Holm, Louis C.K., Barry White, Paul Walker, Ben McKenzie, Jennifer Hudson

13 Claudette Colbert, Roald Dahl, Jacqueline Bisset, Mel Tormé, Tyler Perry, Shane Warne, Stella McCartney, Fiona Apple, Ben Savage, Niall Horan

14 Melissa Leo, Amanda Barrie, Amy Winehouse, Nas, Carmen Kass

15 Oliver Stone, Agatha Christie, Tommy Lee Jones, Jimmy Carr, Sophie Dahl, Prince Harry, Tom Hardy, Heidi Montag, Sommer Ray

16 Lauren Bacall, Peter Falk, B.B. King, Mickey Rourke, Loyd Grossman, David Copperfield, Jennifer Tilly, Marc Anthony, Katie Melua, Nick Jonas, Amy Poehler, Alexis Bledel, Molly Shannon

17 Hank Williams, Anne Bancroft, John Ritter, Roddy McDowall, Cassandra Peterson, Sherrie Hewson, Damon Hill, Alfie Deyes, Brendan O'Carroll, Adriana Karembeu, Cheryl Strayed, Anastacia, Pixie Geldof

18 Greta Garbo, Anne Diamond, Dizzee Rascal, James Gandolfini, Lance Armstrong, Ronaldo, Jada Pinkett Smith, James Marsden, Dee Dee Ramone

19 Cass Elliot, Brian Epstein, Jimmy Fallon, Adam West, Kate Adie, Jeremy Irons, Twiggy, Trisha Yearwood, Jarvis Cocker, Michelle Alves, Zandra Rhodes, Victoria Silvstedt

20 George R.R. Martin, Sophia Loren, Gary Cole, Malachi Kirby, Kristen Johnston

21 Stephen King, Larry Hagman, Leonard Cohen, Bill Murray, Faith Hill, Ricki Lake, Luke Wilson, Liam Gallagher, Nicole Richie, Cheryl Hines, Jason Derulo

22 Tommy Lasorda, Andrea Bocelli, Bonnie Hunt, Scott Baio, Billie Piper, Joan Jett, Richard Fairbrass, Sue Perkins, Tom Felton, Tatiana Maslany, Nick Cave, Bilbo Baggins

23 (Julio Iglesias – born on the cusp, see Q&A)

Q&A Section

• • • • •

Q. What is the difference between a Sun sign and a Star sign?

A. They are the same thing. The Sun spends one month in each of the twelve star signs every year, so if you were born on 1 January, you are a Sun Capricorn. In astronomy, the Sun is termed a star rather than a planet, which is why the two names are interchangeable. The term 'zodiac sign', too, means the same as Sun sign and Star sign and is another way of describing which one of the twelve star signs you are, e.g. Sun Capricorn.

Q. What does it mean if I'm born on the cusp?

A. Being born on the cusp means that you were born on a day when the Sun moves from one of the twelve zodiac signs into the next. However, the Sun doesn't change signs at the same time each year. Sometimes it can be a day earlier or a day later. In the celebrity birthday section of the book, names in brackets mean that this person's birthday falls into this category.

If you know your complete birth data, including the date, time and place you were born, you can find out definitively what Sun sign you are. You do this by either checking an ephemeris (a planetary table) or asking an astrologer. For example, if a baby were born on 20 January 2018, it would be Sun Capricorn if born before 03:09 GMT or Sun Aquarius if born after 03:09 GMT. A year earlier, the Sun left Capricorn a day earlier and entered Aquarius on 19 January 2017, at 21:24 GMT. Each year the time changes are slightly different.

Q. Has my sign of the zodiac changed since I was born?

A. Every now and again, the media talks about a new sign of the zodiac called Ophiuchus and about there now being thirteen signs. This means that you're unlikely to be the same Sun sign as you always thought you were.

This method is based on fixing the Sun's movement to the star constellations in the sky, and is called 'sidereal' astrology. It's used traditionally in India and other Asian countries.

The star constellations are merely namesakes for the twelve zodiac signs. In western astrology, the zodiac is divided into twelve equal parts that are in sync with the seasons. This method is called 'tropical' astrology. The star constellations and the zodiac signs aren't the same.

Astrology is based on a beautiful pattern of symmetry (see Additional Information) and it wouldn't be the same if a thirteenth sign were introduced into the pattern. So never fear, no one is going to have to say their star sign is Ophiuchus, a name nobody even knows how to pronounce!

Q. Is astrology still relevant to me if I was born in the southern hemisphere?

A. Yes, astrology is unquestionably relevant to you. Astrology's origins, however, were founded in the northern hemisphere, which is why the Spring Equinox coincides with the Sun's move into Aries, the first sign of the zodiac. In the southern hemisphere, the seasons are reversed. Babylonian, Egyptian and Greek and Roman astrology are the forebears of modern-day astrology, and all of these civilisations were located in the northern hemisphere.

• • • • •

Q. Should I read my Sun sign, Moon sign and Ascendant sign?

A. If you know your horoscope or you have drawn up an astrology wheel for the time of your birth, you will be aware that you are more than your Sun sign. The Sun is the most important star in the sky, however, because the other planets revolve around it, and your horoscope in the media is based on Sun signs. The Sun represents your essence, who you are striving to become throughout your lifetime.

The Sun, Moon and Ascendant together give you a broader impression of yourself as all three reveal further elements about your personality. If you know your Moon and Ascendant signs, you can read all three books to gain further insight into who you are. It's also a good idea to read the Sun sign book that relates to your partner, parents, children, best friends, even your boss for a better under-standing of their characters too.

Q. Is astrology a mix of fate and free will?

A. Yes. Astrology is not causal, i.e. the planets don't cause things to happen in your life; instead, the two are interconnected, hence the saying 'As above, so below'. The symbolism of the planets' movements mirrors what's happening on earth and in your personal experience of life.

You can choose to sit back and let your life unfold, or you can decide the best course of action available to you. In this way, you are combining your fate and free will, and this is one of astrology's major purposes in life. A knowledge of astrology can help you live more authentically, and it offers you a fresh perspective on how best to make progress in your life.

Q. What does it mean if I don't identify with my Sun sign? Is there a reason for this?

A. The majority of people identify with their Sun sign, and it is thought that one route to fulfilment is to grow into your Sun sign. You do get the odd exception, however.

For example, a Pisces man was adamant that he wasn't at all romantic, mystical, creative or caring, all typical Pisces archetypes. It turned out he'd spent the whole of his adult life working in the oil industry and lived primarily on the sea. Neptune is one of Pisces' ruling planets and god of the sea and Pisces rules all liquids, including oil. There's the Pisces connection.

Q. What's the difference between astrology and astronomy?

A. Astrology means 'language of the stars', whereas astronomy means 'mapping of the stars'. Traditionally, they were considered one discipline, one form of study and they coexisted together for many hundreds of years. Since the dawn of the Scientific Age, however, they have split apart.

Astronomy is the scientific strand, calculating and logging the movement of the planets, whereas astrology is the interpretation of the movement of the stars. Astrology works on a symbolic and intuitive level to offer guidance and insight. It reunites you with a universal truth, a knowingness that can sometimes get lost in place of an objective, scientific truth. Both are of value.

Q. What is a cosmic marriage in astrology?

A. One of the classic indicators of a relation-ship that's a match made in heaven is the union of the Sun and Moon. When they fall close to each other in the same sign in the birth charts of you and your partner, this is called a cosmic marriage. In astrology, the Sun and Moon are the king and queen of the heavens; the Sun is a masculine energy, and the Moon a feminine energy. They represent the eternal cycle of day and night, yin and yang.

Q. What does the Saturn Return mean?

A. In traditional astrology, Saturn was the furthest planet from the Sun, representing boundaries and the end of the universe. Saturn is linked to karma and time, and represents authority, structure and responsibility. It takes Saturn twenty-nine to thirty years to make a complete cycle of the zodiac and return to the place where it was when you were born.

This is what people mean when they talk about their Saturn Return; it's the astrological coming of age. Turning thirty can be a soul-searching time, when you examine how far you've come in life and whether you're on the right track. It's a watershed moment, a reality check and a defining stage of adulthood. The decisions you make during your Saturn Return are crucial, whether they represent endings or new commitments. Either way, it's the start of an important stage in your life path.

Additional Information

• • • • •

The Symmetry of Astrology

There is a beautiful symmetry to the zodiac (see horoscope wheel). There are twelve zodiac signs, which can be divided into two sets of 'introvert' and 'extrovert' signs, four elements (fire, earth, air, water), three modes (cardinal, fixed, mutable) and six pairs of opposite signs.

One of the values of astrology is in bringing opposites together, showing how they complement each other and work together and, in so doing, restore unity. The horoscope wheel represents the cyclical nature of life.

Aries (*March 21–April 19*)
Taurus (*April 20–May 20*)
Gemini (*May 21–June 20*)
Cancer (*June 21–July 22*)
Leo (*July 23–August 22*)
Virgo (*August 23–September 22*)
Libra (*September 23–October 23*)
Scorpio (*October 24–November 22*)
Sagittarius (*November 23–December 21*)
Capricorn (*December 22–January 20*)
Aquarius (*January 21–February 18*)
Pisces (*February 19–March 20*)

ELEMENTS

There are four elements in astrology and three signs allocated to each. The elements are:

fire – Aries, Leo, Sagittarius
earth – Taurus, Virgo, Capricorn
air – Gemini, Libra, Aquarius
water – Cancer, Scorpio, Pisces

What each element represents:

Fire – fire blazes bright and fire types are inspirational, motivational, adventurous and love creativity and play

Earth – earth is grounding and solid, and earth rules money, security, practicality, the physical body and slow living

Air – air is intangible and vast and air rules thinking, ideas, social interaction, debate and questioning

Water – water is deep and healing and water rules feelings, intuition, quietness, relating, giving and sharing

MODES

There are three modes in astrology and four star signs allocated to each. The modes are:

cardinal – Aries, Cancer, Libra, Capricorn
fixed – Taurus, Leo, Scorpio, Aquarius
mutable – Gemini, Virgo, Sagittarius, Pisces

What each mode represents:

Cardinal – The first group represents the leaders of the zodiac, and these signs love to initiate and take action. Some say they're controlling.

Fixed – The middle group holds fast and stands the middle ground and acts as a stable, reliable companion. Some say they're stubborn.

Mutable – The last group is more willing to go with the flow and let life drift. They're more flexible and adaptable and often dual-natured. Some say they're all over the place.

INTROVERT AND EXTROVERT SIGNS/ OPPOSITE SIGNS

The introvert signs are the earth and water signs and the extrovert signs are the fire and air signs. Both sets oppose each other across the zodiac.

The 'introvert' earth and water oppositions are:

- Taurus – • Scorpio
- Cancer – • Capricorn
- Virgo – • Pisces

The 'extrovert' air and fire oppositions are:

- Aries – • Libra
- Gemini – • Sagittarius
- Leo – • Aquarius

THE HOUSES

The houses of the astrology wheel are an additional component to Sun sign horoscopes. The symmetry that is inherent within astrology remains, as the wheel is divided into twelve equal sections, called 'houses'. Each of the twelve houses is governed by one of the twelve zodiac signs.

There is an overlap in meaning as you move round the houses. Once you know the symbolism of all the star signs, it can be fleshed out further by learning about the areas of life represented by the twelve houses.

The houses provide more specific information if you choose to have a detailed birth chart reading.

This is based not only on your day of birth, which reveals your star sign, but also your time and place of birth. Here's the complete list of the meanings of the twelve houses and the zodiac sign they are ruled by:

1 – **Aries:** self, physical body, personal goals

2 – **Taurus:** money, possessions, values

3 – **Gemini:** communication, education, siblings, local neighbourhood

4 – **Cancer:** home, family, roots, the past, ancestry

5 – **Leo:** creativity, romance, entertainment, children, luck

6 – **Virgo:** work, routine, health, service

7 – **Libra:** relationships, the 'other', enemies, contracts

8 – **Scorpio:** joint finances, other people's resources, all things hidden and taboo

9 – **Sagittarius:** travel, study, philosophy, legal affairs, publishing, religion

10 – **Capricorn:** career, vocation, status, reputation

11 – **Aquarius:** friends, groups, networks, social responsibilities

12 – **Pisces:** retreat, sacrifice, spirituality

A GUIDE TO LOVE MATCHES

The star signs relate to each other in different ways depending on their essential nature. It can also be helpful to know the pattern they create across the zodiac. Here's a quick guide that relates to the chapter on Love Matches:

Two Peas In A Pod – the same star sign

Opposites Attract – star signs opposite each other

Soulmates – five or seven signs apart, and a traditional 'soulmate' connection

In Your Element – four signs apart, which means you share the same element

Squaring Up To Each Other – three signs apart, which means you share the same mode

Sexy Sextiles – two signs apart, which means you're both 'introverts' or 'extroverts'

Next Door Neighbours – one sign apart, different in nature but often share close connections